By Nat Gabriel

Celebration Press
Pearson Learning Group

Contents

FERRET FIELD

It was October, the height of soccer season. Ned sat in math class next to his friend Bill, but his mind was *not* on multiplication. "Did you see that goal I kicked on Sunday?" he asked Bill.

"Yeah, it was awesome!" Bill said. "I could've gotten one too, but the ball took a weird bounce at the last minute."

"It's that crummy field," said Ned. "It has too many holes. Ramon tripped last week! I thought for sure he'd broken his arm."

"The new fields over on Ferris Road will be done pretty soon," said Bill.

"It can't be soon enough for me." Ned sighed.

The bell rang, and Bill and Ned walked together to Mr. Burke's science class. They had just started their unit on the environment, and everyone had chosen a topic to research.

Ned was researching oil spills, and Bill had been reading up on solar power. The projects were due in three weeks. But that all changed when Mr. Burke told them about what his dog, Larry, had brought home the night before.

Mr. Burke always had a new story about the puppy he adopted from the pound. "You know how Larry loves to chase anything that runs fast," related Mr. Burke.

"He's never managed to catch a thing—until last night, that is."

"It wasn't a baby bunny, was it?" Sophia whispered.

"Nope, not a bunny. It was something much more unusual. It was a black-footed ferret!"

"Are you sure, Mr. Burke? I don't think that's possible," said Marta, the class expert on everything. The boys rolled their eyes. "I thought I read that black-footed ferrets are extinct in the wild. Are you sure it wasn't just a baby groundhog? Or maybe a chipmunk?"

"They're *believed to be* extinct," said Mr. Burke. "But good for you, Marta. All good scientists question claims like this one. Sometimes it's hard to know for sure when animals or plants are actually extinct."

"Are you positive that what Larry brought home is a black-footed ferret, and not some other kind?" asked Ned.

"I took the ferret over to the wildlife refuge, and they confirmed it," Mr. Burke said. "They were just as amazed as you are!"

"So are you saying your dog killed the last black-footed ferret in the whole world?" Bill asked.

"First of all, I'm glad to report that the ferret isn't dead," said Mr. Burke. "Dr. Charles from the wildlife refuge thinks that in a couple of weeks, she'll be as good as

new. He said it looks as if the ferret may have been hit by a car and stunned. Larry probably found her lying by the side of the road."

"Then what will happen to her once she's better?" Marta asked. "What if she had a nest of babies? They'll never survive! Will the people at the wildlife refuge release her? How will they know where to put her?"

"Calm down, Marta. Dr. Charles called the Wildlife Federation, and they're going to come have a look at her. I'm sure they'll

know how to handle her. As you can imagine, they're pretty excited about Larry's find! And there's more," said Mr. Burke with a smile. "They're going to send a crew of scientists down here to Beaver Run to try to find more ferrets. They'll need some volunteers to help. They wondered if some of you might be interested in working with them on the project!"

There was a sudden chorus of excited voices.

"I'll help!"

"Me, too. I'm really great at finding stuff!"

"I was pretty sure that's how you'd feel," said Mr. Burke. "Actually, I've already told them that instead of researching our environmental projects this month, we're going to be looking for ferrets. We might never have another opportunity like this one! What do you think?"

The class cheered!

So every day after school for the next three weeks, Mr. Burke's science class helped look for ferrets. A woman from the Wildlife Federation came and talked to the class first. She showed some slides and explained that ferrets are nocturnal; they sleep in the daytime and hunt only after dark.

"They like to hunt prairie dogs," the scientist explained. "Since ferrets are just the right size and shape to slither down prairie dog tunnels, that's where you're likely to find them living and hunting. Mounds of dirt mark the openings of these tunnels, so they're usually pretty easy to spot."

As it turned out, Beaver Run, Wyoming, had a lot of prairie dog mounds. Mr. Burke's class decided to help the scientists by mapping all the prairie dog mounds they located.

At least that was the plan.

The next afternoon at Ferris Field, Bill and
Ned looked down at what they knew had to
be a prairie dog hole. "Do you think we
have to tell?" asked Bill. "If they find ferrets
here, that's the end of our new soccer field."

"I don't want to," Ned said gloomily, "but
if we don't, it's sort of like lying. We have
to tell."

The next morning, with low spirits, the
boys got out the supplies and made a map
to show the location of the mound.

Each night a team of scientists chose a location from the maps the students had made and scanned for ferrets with powerful searchlights and binoculars. Sometimes early in the evening a few students and their parents also observed.

Finally their patience was rewarded. One night a tiny head popped up out of a prairie dog hole. A black-footed ferret! Marta and her dad were there when it happened. She was only too happy to tell the class all about it the next morning.

"We saw three black-footed ferrets last night!" she exclaimed. "It was so cool! Dr. Charles said they never would have located them without our map."

Most of the class cheered. Mr. Burke beamed.

"What field were you in?" asked Ned anxiously. He didn't want to hear her answer.

"We were in Ferris Field," said Marta.

Work on Ferris Field stopped immediately. The *Beaver Run Tribune* sent a reporter and a photographer to interview Mr. Burke and his class.

"Ned Marsh and Bill Hamilton were the ones who first spotted the prairie dog holes in Ferris Field," Mr. Burke told the reporter. "They made the map, too."

"You must be very proud!" the reporter said, turning to the boys. "Tell me how you found the holes."

Ned and Bill looked at each other. Sure they felt proud, but mostly they felt sad. The reporter's pen zipped along as the boys explained their find—and their difficult choice.

Two days later the article appeared in the local paper. Everyone in town was excited—everyone, that is, except Ned and Bill and the rest of their soccer team. Mr. Burke posted the article for everyone to read. Marta seemed especially interested, but, of course, her name was in it.

"At least the reporter told about our soccer field problem," Bill said glumly to Ned. "What a bummer. Do you think the ferrets need the whole field? Maybe they could be trapped and moved to another place. They do that sometimes with other animals!"

But the Wildlife Federation didn't want to disturb the ferrets. There would be no soccer on Ferris Field.

Then one day about a week after the article ran, Mr. Burke asked Ned and Bill to stay after class. Marta and her dad were there, too.

"Mr. Garcia has something interesting to tell you boys," he said.

The boys looked at Mr. Garcia. They'd never met him before. He looked a lot like Marta.

"I was interested by that article about the ferret discovery on the new soccer field," he said. "I used to play soccer, too. I loved it!"

He smiled at the boys and continued, "Marta isn't a soccer player, but she reminded me of something. I have a piece of property in town that I'm not using. We've talked it over, and we have decided to donate the property to the town for a new soccer field. I wanted you two to be the first to know!"

Ned and Bill couldn't believe what they were hearing.

"We've looked carefully," said Marta excitedly, "and there are absolutely no signs of prairie dogs or ferrets anyplace on the field. It's nice and level, and I think it will be perfect!"

"Unbelievable!" said Ned in amazement.

"Awesome!" exclaimed Bill. "And thanks, Marta!"

"Still have mixed feelings about finding those ferrets?" asked Mr. Burke.

"No, not at all!" the boys said together.

A Million and One Ways

Gabby stood in front of a bursting-at-the-seams coat closet, looking for a spot for her scooter. "Why can't you just do like everybody else's mother and recycle these things?" Gabby wailed.

"It's just the way I am, Gabby. I can't stand to get rid of things when I know there's still good use left in them," her mother said.

"But plastic milk jugs, Mom?" Gabby pointed to a pile of them on the closet floor. "How are you ever going to use those? I could use this space for my skates and my scooter, you know!"

"Oh, there are a million and one ways to use a plastic milk jug."

Gabby wasn't in the mood to hear it. She tossed her head in disgust, grabbed her backpack and scooter, and went to her room to start her homework.

The next day in school, Gabby's language arts teacher, Mrs. Diaz, told the class about an assignment she had in mind. They'd been reading plays in small groups, which Gabby really enjoyed.

"We're going to write and perform a play for Earth Day," she told them. "It will be our class's special tribute to the earth. Everyone will have something to do. If you don't want to act, there will be plenty of other ways to help."

Gabby's class had been studying the environment in science. They'd learned about the rain forest and other interesting habitats around the world. They'd visited the local recycling plant to see how it worked. They'd read about endangered species, including the peregrine falcon. The bird had made a comeback and was now thriving in a number of cities.

Gabby loved to write, and she really wanted to help write this play. She thought she might like to act in it, too. Or maybe be the director. That would be right up her alley!

"What exactly is this play going to be about?" asked Ralph.

"Well," said Mrs. Diaz, "I'd like to hear your ideas. I'll list them on the chalkboard."

"I think it should be about a giant hole in the ozone that causes the city to burn up like a big marshmallow," suggested Henry, waving his arms excitedly.

Rachel rolled her eyes. "Oh, Henry! Where do you come up with this stuff?"

"Anybody else have a suggestion?" asked Mrs. Diaz. "Rachel? Often it's good to suggest another idea if we disagree with someone else's."

"Well, we could do a play about turning an abandoned lot into a garden. We did that on my block!" said Rachel proudly.

"Or how about a story about a peregrine falcon that's nesting on the windowsill of an apartment building? Like that red-tailed hawk uptown!" suggested Gabby. "For the play, it could be a special bird that can talk about what it's like to be endangered."

"Maybe it could teach people about how to care more about endangered species," added Gabby's friend Ana.

"And then a hole in the ozone comes along and burns up the talking falcon like a . . ."

"That's enough, Henry," interrupted Mrs. Diaz. She added Gabby's idea to the list. "These are both good suggestions. Let's vote for one."

It was a close vote, but Gabby's idea won. After some discussion, everyone except Henry agreed that the idea for the play was a good one.

That afternoon the class started work on the outline of the play. They knew it had to include a problem and a solution, plenty of action, and some interesting information. Fifteen kids wanted to act in the play.

Gabby had lots of good ideas. So did Ana and Ralph. All week they worked together until finally they had a script with 15 roles. They decided to call it *Peregrine Paradise.*

The next step was to choose parts for the play. They chose Ana to play the falcon because she took ballet and would make a graceful bird. There were several other bird characters, and someone had to be the falcon's prey.

Some characters helped the falcon by feeding it and protecting it from a grumpy old man who wanted to use its feathers for fishing lures. They picked Henry to be the grumpy old man. Gabby would play the part of the bird-watcher who discovers the bird's nest.

"We'll need 15 different costumes," Sally said. She offered to ask her mother to help, since they had a sewing machine at home.

"What about scenery?" Gabby asked. "We have two different settings—the windowsill and the park. That could be tricky!"

"Actually, Gabby, your mother called this morning to volunteer to help with that," smiled Mrs. Diaz. "I told her I thought that would be great. You're right—the scenery will be tricky."

"She did?" Gabby was surprised. She had been talking about the play all week, but her mother hadn't mentioned wanting to help with the scenery. Gabby thought she might at least have *asked* her before calling Mrs. Diaz!

"Are you really going to help make the scenery for our play, Mom?" Gabby asked when her mom got home from work that night. "You never told me!" Gabby was a little nervous about what her mother might have in mind.

"Well, I'd like to. I've been thinking about it ever since you told me about the play, and I think I have some ideas that might work and would be fun to do."

"Like what?" asked Gabby suspiciously.

"You'll see. I'm going to meet with the class tomorrow," Mrs. Mehta said with a little smile. That's all she would say no matter how much Gabby coaxed her.

The next day Mrs. Mehta stopped at school on her way to work to talk to the class about the scenery. "I'm going to need a lot of help," she told them.

"I'm a pretty good artist," Henry told her, "especially if you happen to need some pictures of explosions and stuff like that."

"Actually," said Mrs. Mehta, "the kind of help I need right now won't require you to be good artists, just good collectors."

Gabby couldn't figure out what her mother was talking about. How could the kids help make scenery by being good collectors? She was beginning to wonder if she really wanted her mother to help with this play.

"We're going to be making our scenery out of things you might otherwise recycle," Mrs. Mehta explained.

"You mean like . . . *garbage*?" Henry asked.

"No," Mrs. Mehta laughed. "I mean things like cardboard paper-towel tubes, jar lids, and especially . . . "

Gabby closed her eyes. She knew what was coming. She just wanted to disappear.

" . . . plastic milk jugs," her mom said. "You can use them in a million and one ways!"

"Won't it look kind of, well, junky?" Ana asked, trying to sound polite.

"Have you ever seen bold, colorful flowers made from milk jugs, or a gorgeous sun made out of jar lids? They are positively beautiful!" Mrs. Mehta declared.

Several of the kids snickered.

Gabby jumped up and ran out of the room. She'd never been so embarrassed in her life. How could her mother have done this to her? Everyone would make fun of her now because her mother was so strange.

Gabby sat on the floor in front of her locker with her head buried in her arms. She tried not to cry. Soon Mrs. Diaz found her there. She knelt down beside Gabby and spoke to her gently.

"Gabby, talk to me. Tell me what's wrong," Mrs. Diaz said.

"You wouldn't understand," Gabby sniffed. "You don't have a mother who loves garbage and who goes around telling all your friends about it."

"No, but I don't have the kind of mother who ever volunteered to help out with a school play either," she said.

"I don't want her to help!" Gabby cried. "Not if it means everyone in the class thinks she's weird! Why can't she be like everyone else and make normal scenery out of paper and paint?"

"Listen, Gabby. Most people probably would make scenery out of those things. But do you remember when you did the rain forest project earlier this year in science class?"

Gabby nodded.

"You learned what a difference it would make if people found ways to use less paper," Mrs. Diaz said, "and how plastics pollute the water and fill our landfills to overflowing."

Gabby nodded and sniffed.

"I think that your mother's idea to recycle things to make scenery is a terrific way to show that we really care about the earth."

Gabby listened politely. But she felt Mrs. Diaz just didn't understand.

"You don't get it!" she said. "Recycling is great! We do it at home. But we want our scenery for the play to look really cool! Sometimes I think Mom still thinks we're all little kids. We can make *real* scenery! Mom should've told me she was coming to do this—I would've talked her out of it."

Mrs. Diaz smiled. "Gabby, your mother volunteered to help, and we can certainly use her help. Why don't you just wait and see what she has in mind? You might be surprised."

"I've had enough surprises already today," Gabby sniffed. "I'll act in the play, but I don't want to have anything to do with the scenery."

"It's up to you," said Mrs. Diaz. "I'm sure your mom would really like to have you help out, but I know the rest of the group can manage just fine."

A week later the class was setting up the scenery for the opening of the play. Mrs. Mehta had taken the morning off to help, and things were not going well. The trees kept tipping over. The jar lids kept falling off of the sun.

The bird's nest, made from recycled twine, somehow ended up on Henry's head. Gabby grabbed it away, and the nest immediately self-destructed. Gabby thought she was going to self-destruct, too. She fled to the girls' room.

The kids in the primary school were coming with their parents to see the show at 2:00. Somehow by 1:00 most of the scenery was in place, and it was time to get into costume. Actually, the costumes looked terrific— and, although Gabby didn't know it, the stage had been totally transformed.

Giant silvery blossoms made of plastic milk jugs hung on paper-towel-tube stems while a giant sun, made from a hundred jar lids, glittered overhead. Groves of carpet-roll trees swayed, and bark-chip paths wandered through a field planted with "grass" straight from the school paper shredder. Fluffy clouds made from packing peanuts hung in the sky.

"Places, please!" called Mrs. Diaz. "Has anyone seen Gabby?"

No one had any idea where Gabby was, but the show could not wait. When the curtain went up, the audience gasped and applauded. Gabby crept backstage. Her mother was standing in the dark, watching. Gabby looked at the stage. It looked unbelievable! The audience loved the play already, and it hadn't even started!

"Listen to that, Mom," Gabby whispered. "They're clapping for the scenery. They're clapping for you." Her mother hugged her.

Peregrine's Paradise was a total success. Ana's falcon was so graceful it actually seemed to be airborne. Henry was so good as the grumpy old man his own mother scarcely recognized him. Gabby the bird-watcher appeared, amazingly, right out of the audience, looking through her binoculars in search of the peregrine falcon!

After the play, Mrs. Diaz had all the children gather to thank Mrs. Mehta for the wonderful job she'd done. Henry stepped forward and cleared his throat.

"Mrs. Mehta, you told us that there are a million and one ways to use a milk jug, but did you think of this one?"

From behind his back Henry pulled a crown he had made out of a plastic milk jug. There were small, colored bottle caps glued all around it like colorful gems. He placed the crown on Mrs. Mehta's head and declared, "Three cheers for the queen of recycling!"

No one cheered louder than Gabby.

Greenies

It seemed as if nobody at my new school ever thought about the environment. They didn't mind wasting paper or water or anything else. It drove me absolutely crazy. My parents were big on not wasting resources.

On the first day of school, I brought my lunch in a lunchbox, with a thermos, a cloth napkin, and a metal fork and spoon, just as I had done at my old school.

"Serena, people at Greenville Elementary just don't use those things," Jenny Baum told me. Jenny was the first person to help me. She was trying to "show me the ropes." "We use juice boxes, not thermoses. Cloth napkins are not cool, and lunchboxes are for little kids."

I was lonely. I wanted to fit in, but I really didn't want to hurt the environment.

"Mom, what about packing my lunch in a paper bag from now on?" I asked after that first day in the lunchroom.

"Paper bags are a waste, honey. You know that. I'd like to think we're helping to save a tree every time I pack your lunchbox," she answered.

I didn't even bother to ask what she thought about plastic forks. I knew, and I agreed with her. Why should we make mountains of garbage just so we can toss out our plasticware? It doesn't make sense.

Jenny Baum tried explaining how things were done in Greenville a few more times, and then she gave up on me. She didn't ask me if I wanted to sit with her at lunch anymore, so I decided to find a seat somewhere else. I can just guess what she would think if she knew about the worms.

Now we live in a townhouse with a tiny backyard. But at my old house we had a big compost heap in the backyard where we put all the vegetable peelings and stuff like that. Mom loves to garden. She calls compost "garden gold." But there's no room for a compost heap here.

On her birthday my mother opened a big box from my father. "What in the world?" she exclaimed. The word *WORMS* was on the box.

"It's an indoor compost heap!" Dad explained. "You can put all the stuff that goes in an outdoor compost heap right in this box with the earthworms. The tiny holes let air in but are too small for the worms to crawl out."

Mom was thrilled. She put the box under the sink, and those worms started making "garden gold" right away.

When my birthday came in October, my mother asked if I'd like to invite a few friends over.

"I don't have a few friends, Mom," I said. "In fact, I don't have *any* friends. I just don't fit in here. Nobody else is like me."

"Be patient, Serena," she said as she brushed my hair back. "You just haven't found your place yet. When you do, you'll make friends in no time at all. I guarantee it."

I wanted to believe her, but I wasn't so sure that Mom was right. I didn't tell anybody at school that Tuesday was my birthday. In the morning, while Mom made my favorite breakfast, pancakes with raspberry syrup, my father gave me a birthday gift—a solar-powered calculator.

"Neat, Daddy. Thanks!"

"That doesn't mean you can't work on your math on cloudy days," he told me with a wink. "Then you might have to plug it in." Mom brought in the pancakes. There were 10 candles on top. "Make a wish, Serena!"

I closed my eyes and wished hard.

Please, please let me find just one person around here to be my friend.

On the way to school that morning I noticed something I'd never seen before. One of the houses nearby had a strange-looking structure on top of the roof. It was made of glass, and the sun glinted off it.

"Do you know what that is?" a voice behind me asked.

I turned around and saw that it was a girl from my school. I didn't know her name, but I had seen her on the school playground.

"It's a solar panel," she explained. "It heats the water we use."

I was going to say how cool that was, but then I stopped.

"Remember, this is Greenville," I said to myself. "Maybe she thinks having a solar panel is weird, not cool."

42

"I'm Serena," I said as we started walking.

"I know," she said, "You're the new girl in Class 4-D who brings her lunch in a lunchbox."

I felt my face turning red. "Paper bags waste trees," I said. "But nobody around here seems to care."

"Don't be too sure," she said. She opened her backpack and pulled out an old metal lunchbox. "This was my dad's," she said. "We've been saving trees for a long time!"

43

"Wow! Was that really your dad's lunchbox?" I asked, feeling very pleased.

"Yep. That's the Beatles on there," she said. "Oh, I'm Alice, by the way, Alice Burns."

Alice and I walked all the way to school together. When we got there, she went to classroom 4-B, and I went to my classroom down the hall. Later, at lunch break, I looked for her.

"Hi," I said, sitting down in the empty chair next to her.

"Welcome to the green table," she answered.

I looked at the table. It was the same color as all the other tables in the room—brown. "What do you mean?" I asked.

Just then a boy and two more girls joined us.

"Hey, Alice," the boy said. "Who's this?"

"This is Serena," said Alice.

"Does she want to eat with us?" asked one of the girls.

"Let's give her the test!" said Alice.

Give me the test? I didn't like the sound of that! Then Alice pulled my lunchbox over in front of her. What was she doing?

She took out my thermos and the rest of my lunch, including the cloth napkin. Then she waved the napkin above her head like a flag.

"Wow, cloth! I guess she passes the test!" said the boy.

"This is George," Alice said, introducing us. "Mary, Vera, this is Serena. She's new in town, and as you can see, she's *very* green."

"It's nice to meet a fellow greenie," said Vera.

I didn't know what to say. Alice looked over at me. "You do know what *greenie* means, don't you?"

"Sure I know," I said. "It stands for people who want to save the trees and other natural resources. I'm just, well, surprised to find so many of you here. I thought I was the only one."

"No way. There are lots of us. We even have a club," George said with a laugh. "Ms. Mundee is our advisor."

After school I walked home with Alice.

"Do you want to come over?" she asked. "You could stay for dinner."

"I'd like to. Really. But I've got to be home for dinner because it's . . . my birthday."

"Really? How come you didn't say so? We don't sing 'Happy Birthday' because we sing so badly it would be noise pollution." Alice giggled. "But we could have stuck a candle in your sandwich."

I smiled. I liked Alice. I liked her a lot.

That night after dinner I followed my mother to the kitchen.

"Scoot, will you?" she said. "I'm going to put the candles on your cake so you can have another wish."

"I don't need any candles, Mom," I said.

"Why not?" she asked.

Just then the doorbell rang.

"Serena!" my father called from the other room.

When I went out into the living room, Alice, Mary, Vera, and George were there.

"Happy birthday!" they cried.

"I don't need any more candles," I said to my mother, "because my wish has already come true."